THE EDGE OF KNOWN REALITY AND BEYOND

JONATHAN SKINNER

THE EDGE OF KNOWN REALITY AND BEYOND

GOD, LIFE, THE UNIVERSE

 EVANGELICAL PRESS

 **EVANGELICAL PRESS**

EVANGELICAL PRESS
Faverdale North Industrial Estate, Darlington, DL3 0PH England
e-mail: sales@evangelicalpress.org

Evangelical Press USA
PO Box 825, Webster, NY 14580 USA
e-mail: usa.sales@evangelicalpress.org

www.evangelicalpress.org

A wide range of excellent books on spiritual subjects is available from
Evangelical Press. Please write to us for a free catalogue or contact us
by e-mail. Full details are also available on our web site.

First published 2005

British Library Cataloguing in Publication Data available

Printed and bound in Great Britain by Creative Print & Design Wales,
Ebbw Vale

ISBN-13 978 0 85234 600 6   ISBN 0 85234 600 X

Table of Contents

For Julia

And to our children, Libby, Tom, Henry and Susannah,
whose thoughtful and profound questions originally
brought this book into being.

Introduction: The Big Q

It seems to be basic to being human to wonder if there is any-thing more to life — more than just making the most of the seventy or so years that our hearts manage to keep beating.

Our lives are all too brief. In fact, the sad truth is that we only keep together the atoms that make us *us* for about 650,000 hours. 650,000 hours — that's nothing! After that these faith-ful friendly atoms, which have configured together to make our bodies, lose their sense of loyalty and begin to find other com-mitments. Our lives are too short.

But not only are our lives frighteningly short, they can often feel tragically pointless. After all, what is the purpose of such a short existence? What is the point of being courageous, or good, or kind, if all we end up as is being dissipated into nothingness? If we are merely freaky bundles of molecules that just happen to possess conscious thought for a few hours then there is no real significance or point to anything we do. It's like an absurd cos-mic joke — we have climbed, clambered and evolved far enough out of some primeval sludge to achieve conscious thought only to become conscious enough to comprehend that our fleeting existences are futile.

What is life all about? How can we make sense of it? Where have we come from? Why are we here?

This reflecting seems to be unique to us. Do you ever see a monkey meditating on the meaning of life? Has anyone ever stumbled over a python pontificating on the possibility of con-tinued consciousness after death? Indeed, can you conceive of a kangaroo cogitating whether its existence is worthwhile? Of course not — as far as we know it is only homo sapiens, that is, people, who think like this. We are uniquely conscious beings

— and that unique consciousness makes us think — and sometimes it makes us really think.

At some time or another, most of us engage our brains on the really big questions of life, death, the universe — and beyond. Whether we are moved to ponder by a sunset or jolted into reflection by the sudden death of a friend we start, for a moment, to shake off the shroud of indifference that our society pulls over us and seriously begin to wonder. And it is this sort of wondering we are about to explore. So, tune in your cerebral cortex, switch on your neuronal connections, take a deep breath and let's set out on a mental journey to the edge of known reality — and beyond.

As we begin our adventure of exploration and discovery into the unknown, and decide to stretch our mental machinery to beyond its capacity, it is important to ask what the really big questions are. After all, if we don't know the questions we are asking, it will hardly be surprising if we stumble over less-than-clear answers.

We could list a whole series of critical questions: Is there any real significance to my life? Does it matter how I behave? Does it matter whether I am kind or cruel? — Whether I help an old granny across the road, or push her under a bus? Are these seven or so decades all I have? Is that it? Does my consciousness persist after my body's atoms dissipate when my body finally staggers to a biological halt and then either slowly rots or quickly burns? These are urgent questions and we haven't got long to find the answers. The countdown to possible oblivion is well advanced. We had better get a move on.

What may be helpful is to find some sort of key to unlock this box of conundrums and sort them into some kind of sense. The key may be to discover the question behind the questions, to uncover the question behind all questions. But is there such an ultimate all consuming, all connecting question. I think there is.

Now don't turn off when I say this, but I think it is the old 'God Question'. Let me explain. If there is no God and we are just a random collaboration of molecules that somehow mindlessly stumbles upon conscious thought, then chance rules. By chance, we wake from cosmic nothingness only to dream for a while before entering our short nightmare: oblivion. If this is the case, then there is no significance to my life; it does not ultimately matter how I behave — and there is nothing after death.

On the other hand, if there is a God, the supreme personal ruler of the universe and beyond, then I am made for a purpose. I am watched as to how I behave and my life will extend beyond the grave. I am accountable. Of course, it all depends on what that God is like and how he has made the universe — and we can only know these things if he has communicated them to us. But these secondary issues will have to wait — they can only be answered once we accept that God exists. We will return to whether he has spoken and how he may have set up the whole of reality later. First things must come first.

For now, it is sufficient to say the existence of God at least holds out the possibility of purpose, an understanding of what is good and what is bad, and whether there is life after death. So, the first and key question, the Big Question, if you will, is 'Does God Exist?'

*The universe is not only queerer than we suppose;
it is queerer than we can suppose.*

J. B. S. Haldane, Biologist

Follow the White Rabbit

So, the key question is, 'Does God exist?' Many believe he doesn't, and feel that any belief in something like that should be relegated to the nursery. Faith in God is seen as an illusion — wishful thinking for the gullible and a vain dream for the weak minded.

However, many who take this position have never really looked carefully at the evidence; they have hardened opinions based on little more than ignorance and prejudice. A few have reacted against a Christian upbringing and have never seriously looked back since their childhood or teenage rejection. Others have been raised in homes with a mindset against any Christian perspective; they have swallowed the pill of cynicism without critical thought. The majority, perhaps, fall between these more extreme backgrounds and have assimilated the indifference and scepticism of our society. Agnosticism rules — we don't know — we can't know — and there is no point in even trying to know.

The fact of the matter is that many who hold each of these varying perspectives have never really considered the evidence seriously. Nor have they considered it with an open mind. I'm not saying this is deliberate. There just isn't time. Higher priorities lift us off our feet and propel us in other directions. But for those who can press life's pause button for a few moments, we will steer a course straight into the key cosmic question: Is there anyone out there? Does God exist?

For those who set out on such a journey, this might well, depending on your perception, be a mind-altering exercise — and, even mind-bending. It will certainly lead down pathways of understanding that may rupture your perception of life, reality and

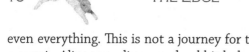

even everything. This is not a journey for the faint-hearted. As a certain Alice once discovered, rabbit holes can go a lot deeper than you think.

So, what evidence is there that there is a God?[1] The best place to start is right where we are, looking at what we see around us. If we carefully consider what we encounter every day, we will uncover some important clues, clues that might even totally change the way we think. Strangely, the obvious isn't always the most obvious. Rabbit holes often begin right where we are standing — we can trip over them.

From Snooker to Dominoes

We live in a world where nothing happens by itself; things only occur because something else causes them to occur. Nothing is truly autonomous. Think of snooker balls for instance: a coloured ball rolls across the table and into a corner pocket. Why does this happen? It takes place because a white ball sped across the tabletop and hit the coloured ball. So, the coloured ball only moved because of the force of the white ball bumping into it. But then we logically ask: why did the white ball move so that it crashed into the coloured one? And of course the answer is because it was hit by the cue. And then the cue moved because the player moved it; the player moved his arms because of the contraction of his muscles. But it does not stop there: the muscles contracted due to chemical reactions in the cells and so produced that movement. And the chemical reactions caused the movement because they were releasing chemical energy they had received from the blood. And where did the blood get its energy? This was absorbed through the intestinal wall from food that had been digested. But this is not the end of the story either: the food received its energy from the sun. Either the food was plant matter, or it was meat from an animal that originally ate plants. Whichever way we look at it, all our energy comes from the sun. The millions of green leaves we see around us are silently and gently processing the beams of sunlight that fall on them. And some of those plants are considerate enough to store that energy in a form that is palatable and digestible — in short, they feed us and keep us alive.

But all this is only the start of the journey. If we think about the sun we realise that it does not make energy out of nowhere; it simply releases it from the chemicals it is made of. The next obvious question is where did these substances get their energy? They received them from elsewhere, from somewhere else in space. Energy flows through the cosmos but where does it come from? The rabbit hole keeps going, but now it bends out of view. From here on we can only guess — with a little help from cosmologists. The main point is clear though: nothing happens by itself. It only happens because something happens to it.

In other words, what we see all around is what scientists call 'cause and effect'. Something acts on something else to produce a result or effect. Whatever we look at had something causing it, which in turn had something causing it, and that in turn had something causing it. And like a tumbling line of dominoes, the chain reaction can't be infinite. This chain of cause and effect intriguingly disappears out of sight. It is the White Rabbit going down a rather deep and mysteriously fascinating burrow.

Another way of expressing this is to say that everything is dependent on something else; nothing acts by itself. Nothing is autonomous. Some scientists and philosophers use a special word for this — contingent. In a former generation, if a young woman was asked out for a walk in the park, she might well have said something like, 'I would be pleased to go, contingent upon the weather.' In today's speech, what she meant was, 'I will go, dependent upon the weather.' Contingent means dependent.

The point of all this is that everything in our universe is contingent; everything is dependent; everything is bound up in a relationship of cause and effect. The natural question that arises out of this is what caused the whole process? What started it all

off? You can't have contingencies going back for ever; you can't have an endless chain of causes. There has to be a First Cause. There has to be something (or perhaps someone) that started it all.

The universe as we experience it is made of dependent stuff. This means that any hunk of it that we bump up against is unable to explain itself — we must appeal beyond it to something else to explain it. No single element of our world is self-explanatory. This is true of every part of our universe; but also, if you take the universe as a whole, the whole thing is contingent. Everything in our universe is contingent, or dependent, and therefore the whole universe must be contingent. If you have a whole load of contingencies and put them together, you don't suddenly get an explanation, you get a lot of contingency. A universe full of contingent stuff is a contingent universe. If all the parts are dependent, then the totality must be dependent. But what is it all dependent on? Where has the White Rabbit gone?

Where has the White Rabbit Gone?

Logically, the universe must be dependent on something non-dependent. By definition the cause must be non-contingent — something outside of our contingent and dependent universe must have caused it. This perspective is consistent with what the Bible opens with, and teaches throughout. Genesis 1:1 puts it in these words: 'In the beginning God created the heavens and the earth.' This independent reality might just be the God described in the Bible.

Sometimes people respond to this by asking the question, 'Well then, if that is true, who made God?' And the answer is of course that nothing made God, because God by definition is independent or non-contingent. The whole argument for his existence here is based on the need for something autonomous or absolute — something that everything else is dependent upon

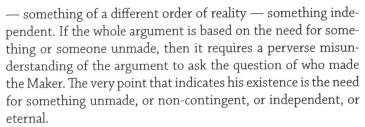

— something of a different order of reality — something independent. If the whole argument is based on the need for something or someone unmade, then it requires a perverse misunderstanding of the argument to ask the question of who made the Maker. The very point that indicates his existence is the need for something unmade, or non-contingent, or independent, or eternal.

When scientists gather their data they try to come up with a theory or model that fits and explains the evidence. Various theories might be suggested, and then the best one is picked — the one that is most consistent with the data. What the Bible gives us is a model or theory as to how to view the universe: the universe is dependent on what it calls 'God', who is independent of it. All the evidence that we have been looking at is consistent with this perspective. That is not the same as saying that this evidence proves the existence of God — that would be stretching the data too far, making it prove more than it is able to bare. But it is quite fair to say that belief in God is consistent with this data. The White Rabbit might well lead to God.

The question that arises is whether there are other theories that fit the evidence better. Some people have suggested that an all-powerful absolute Creator is not needed, all that is required is something more powerful that anything in our purely material cosmos. They say that such a force or being could have set the ball rolling, so speak. But of course this can't be true, for by definition what is needed is something independent or non-contingent — that is, absolute. If the something that made our universe was immensely powerful, but still dependent or contingent, then we would have to ask, well, what caused it? In other words, it would not solve the problem of a dependent universe. The only way a contingent universe could come into being is by something non-contingent, or absolute. Anything just a bit more powerful, be it a force or being, would not fit the bill. This theory is not consistent with the evidence.

The Magicians

This neatly knocks on the head many of the pagan, neo-pagan or new age perspectives that are so rife these days. One has only to peruse the average bookshop to realize how a belief in some spiritual force, forces, or even gods has captured the hearts and minds of many. Most of the alternative therapies have at root an acceptance of this sort of thing. Indeed, this shift of popular thinking in an ever-increasing belief of this kind is upheld by one survey that found that British people are becoming less religious but more spiritual.[2] What was meant by religious was something controlling, institutional and moralizing; what was understood by spiritual was the appreciation of another dimension to life beyond the merely material and mechanistic.

Pagan, neo-pagan, or new age followers feel that the cosmos is caused by gods or forces, who although powerful are not absolutely powerful — they are dependent beings, and as such still need an explanation themselves. For those who feel that 'God' is the force behind and within nature in all its manifestations, then the same problem still arises. Those who take this perspective feel that there is no real distinction between nature and 'God', for the force not only infuses nature, but is one with nature.[3] The problem here is that if the 'god-force' is indistinct from nature, then 'it' or 'he' or 'she', depending on the particular perspective, is by definition dependent. This understanding has a contingent force within and behind the cosmos — and such a force still needs a non-contingent cause.

Whichever way we look at the pagan model or theory, it does not fit with a contingent universe. Again, the biblical perspective is consistent with the data: a creator-God who is independent and non-contingent explains the universe as we experience it: 'In the beginning God created the heavens and the earth.'

It is interesting and significant that at the time of the early spread of Christianity recorded in the New Testament, one of the main arguments used against paganism was the need and reality of an independent creator-God. This is recorded in Acts 14:15: 'We are bringing you good news, telling you to turn from these worthless things to the living God, who made heaven and earth and the sea and everything in them.' The man who said this, the Apostle Paul, used the same approach when he was debating with the Greek philosophers in Athens in Acts 17:24-28:

> *The God who made the world and everything in it is the Lord of heaven and earth and does not live in temples built by hands. And he is not served by human hands, as if he needed anything, because he himself gives all men life and breath and everything else. From one man he made every nation of men, that they should inhabit the whole earth; and he determined the times set for them and the exact places where they should live. God did this so that men would seek him and perhaps reach out for him and find him, though he is not far from each of us.*

The Stuffers

But even though a modern 'spiritual', new age, or neo-pagan perspective does not fit the evidence of a contingent universe, are there other models that fit better, or at least as well as a belief in the one creator-God described in the Bible? Many people feel there is — and they are the Stuffers. The Stuffers are people who only believe in stuff. To put it another way, they only believe that matter exists, and so are more often called 'materialists'. The Stuffers feel that although everything we see is contingent, and it might therefore imply a non-contingent cause, the reality of the situation is that matter has always existed. The cause and effect relationships of contingency just keep on going back for ever — for no less than infinity. Stuff is eternal. But the stuffers have a problem here, and it is a very big problem — in fact, as big as the universe. Their problem is that they have run out of

time — just like the White Rabbit running past Alice muttering 'Oh dear! Oh dear! I shall be late.'

The universe only has so much available energy in it and it is running down. Scientists have what they call 'the Second Law of Thermodynamics'. Basically, this law describes the universe the way we experience it, that is, that available energy is getting less and less. If this fundamental law is true, and no reputable scientist would dispute it, then according to the Stuffers we would have already run out of energy. If the universe has been going on for ever, and if it only has a certain amount of energy, and that is being continually used up, then clearly it should have run out by now. But as the energy of the universe is still running down, then clearly our cosmos must have had a beginning. The universe cannot be eternal; this stuff must have had a beginning.

It might be helpful to think of a car. If a car is driving along a road with a full tank of petrol, and if there are no garages, there will come a point when it will run out of fuel. If there was only a certain amount of petrol in the tank in the first place and no more could be added, and also it was continually being used up to the point that is stopped, then it is obvious that there was a time when the journey started. It would be illogical and absurd to think that the journey had been going on for ever. In the same way, it would be equally illogical and absurd to suppose that a universe with a limited amount of available energy has always been here — it hasn't. There are no cosmic petrol stations. To put it in a sentence: our dependent or contingent universe must have had a beginning when what it was contingent on made it.

However, most Stuffers don't capitulate at this point; they fall back to another line of defence. The most common view these days for the beginning of the universe is some form of the Big Bang theory. Put simply, this says that the whole universe started as a microscopically and infinitesimally tiny dot. This dot was apparently so small that it had no dimensions — it is known as a singularity. From this jot, a Big Bang of cosmic proportions apparently ensued, the result of which is all that we can see, hear, smell, taste and feel — everything we can detect with our most advanced technology — and all we can't detect as well. Whether this theory is true or not does not really affect the argument we are sketching out for the existence of God. If this was the way the universe came into being then that singularity was still contingent — where on earth (I'm sure that's not the right way of expressing this) did that come from? So with or without a Big Bang we still need an explanation for a contingent and dependent universe. The power of the argument remains.

But the point the Stuffers make here is not the case for such a Big Bang, but what happened before the Big Bang. Their next argument for a universe that is eternal and does not need an explanation is that before the Big Bang there was another universe — the opposite of our expanding and running down one. This contracting cosmos ended up crashing and falling in on itself to form the singularity. What they imagine happening is what is sometimes called a steady-state universe, which is oscillating or continually contracting and expanding. So, our universe expands and runs down until it has expanded and run down so much that it is evenly spread out through space. At this point the forces of expansion are overcome by gravity and this starts to pull it together again, until we end up with the singularity, which then explodes, expands and runs down again. By proposing this neat scheme of things some Stuffers feel they have comprehended an eternal universe that is itself non-contingent and not dependent on anything or anyone else. If this is true the argument of contingency breaks down. The White Rabbit has disappeared down a blind burrow — it leads nowhere. (Or, perhaps more accurately, it leads back up to the surface again.)

But however ingenious this idea is, we have to ask a pretty tough question. And the question is this: what evidence is there for such an oscillating universe? Here, the emperor of stuffism is seen as embarrassingly stark naked. It all sounds very clever, but all it is, is an imaginative bit of fantasy — there is not one piece of evidence in its favour — it is all guesswork — a leap of faith, if you will (or wishful thinking). All we see is a universe that is expanding and running down, and so it is pure conjecture to imagine that it was preceded and will be followed by one that is contracting and increasing in energy. There is a basic law of science and philosophy that should be brought to bear here. And it is this: if something looks like a cucumber, smells like a cucumber and tastes like a cucumber, then the burden of proof lies with those who would say that it is not a cucumber. Blind faith will not do.

There is still another problem with asking what was before the Big Bang — and things now get really peculiar, or as Alice said when down the rabbit hole, 'Curiouser and curiouser!' It is actually utterly meaningless to ask what happened before the Big Bang. The reason for this is that scientists call the point of singularity $t = 0$, that is, this is when time began. Before $t = 0$, time didn't exist. There was no 'before' to enquire into; there was no past to emerge from. That's what the physicists say — and that's where their calculations lead. What is needed, therefore, is something or someone outside of time, or eternal, to bring it into being.[4] Again, this is entirely consistent with the biblical perspective, 'In the beginning God created the heavens and the earth.' And it is totally inconsistent with the fantasy of 'Once upon a time'. There was no time.

Putting all this together, when we look carefully at the universe around us, we see everything is contingent, or dependent. This is the White Rabbit. And when, like Alice, we follow the White Rabbit, we find ourselves going down a trail to something beyond our imagination. The trail or burrow of cause and effect leads to someone or something uncaused, independent or non-contingent. There is no way out.

This does not prove the existence of God as such, but it is certainly consistent with belief in God. What is intriguing is that it does seem to rule out the opinion that our universe is self-explanatory. All the evidence fits the God-model.

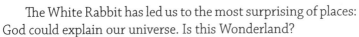

The White Rabbit has led us to the most surprising of places: God could explain our universe. Is this Wonderland?

Of course, in the original tale, Alice was only dreaming, but there again, as Morpheus asked in the film, *The Matrix*, 'Have you ever had a dream Neo, that you were so sure was real? What if you were unable to wake from that dream? How would you know the difference between the dream world and the real world?'

Perhaps the dream is that there is no White Rabbit — and no Wonderland — and most people are asleep.

Perhaps reality truly is stranger than fiction.

Perhaps the Bible could wake us up to see the universe as it really is — and more importantly, who is behind it.

Perhaps behind this universe there is someone — someone who makes sense of everything.

To quote *The Matrix* again: 'The truth is out there.'

The more I examine the universe and study the details of its architecture, the more evidence I find that the universe in some sense must have known we were coming.

Freeman Dyson

Down the Burrow

So far, we have followed the White Rabbit down the burrow of cause and effect, and noted that where this leads is totally consistent with belief in God. It leads to something non-dependent, or non-contingent — and this could well be the God described in the Bible.

I say 'could well' because for each of us our word 'God' is stuffed full of various meanings, and this non-contingent reality behind the universe does not necessarily have to fit any of our personal guesses or opinions. In other words, although something exists behind the universe we are at this point still very much in the dark about what that something or someone is. More is needed — much more.

In order to get a better idea, what we need to do now is to back-track a little from where the White Rabbit and its burrow lead (the non-contingent cause) and actually take some time to examine the length of the burrow itself. The burrow, as we have said, is the chain of causes and effects that runs through everything in our universe. It is the universe itself.

As we look at this burrow of contingencies, perhaps the most striking thing is how utterly unlikely it is that we should be here considering it at all. If, as many believe, everything is the result of a massive series of phenomenal cosmic accidents, then we are the most outrageous fluke imaginable. In terms of probability, we shouldn't be here. It almost seems like magic — unbelievably, the exact conditions suitable for sustaining life were generated — and then life itself appeared. It is like a magician pulling a rabbit out of a hat — but perhaps there is more here than meets the eye.

Can a White Rabbit Really Be Pulled Out of a Hat?

Are we the result of a cosmic coincidence? Is our life-sustaining universe merely the fall-out of an arbitrary accident? Some scientists don't think so. We all take gravity for granted — but the physicist Brandon Carter has pointed out the staggering discovery that if the strength of this force, which keeps our feet on the ground, were altered by even a miniscule amount, then 'stars like our sun would not exist'.[1] And another scientist, Edward Kolb, interviewed by Newsweek magazine said, 'It turns out that the "constants of nature", such as the strength of gravity, have exactly the values that allows stars and planets to form... The universe, it seems, is fine-tuned to let life and consciousness flower.'[2] The question is, can this be explained by blind, random chance, or is this not an accident at all?

But this is not the only 'fluke' in our universe that allows life. Another concerns atoms, the basic building blocks of matter. Scientists have now discovered that if the force that holds them together were even slightly weaker, the whole universe would have consisted of nothing but hydrogen gas. But if, on the other hand, it had been even a little stronger, the stars could not have formed. Stephen Hawkins, the famous professor at Cambridge concludes: 'It seems clear that there are relatively few ranges of values for the numbers that would allow the development of any form of intelligent life.'[3]

Another staggering statistic is that the particles called protons inside our atoms are apparently 1,836 times more massive than electrons. Now that may not feel staggering, but if that number were slightly different, then there would be no chemistry of life, no page in front of you, and — not to put too fine of a point on it — no you. Again Stephen Hawkins comments that this seems 'to have been very finely adjusted to make possible the development of life'.[4] All this begs a simple question: If this really is fine-tuning — who, or what, did it?

I know it may sound like something out of Star Trek or the X-files, but apparently there really is a substance called 'antimatter'. Scientists have made it in their laboratories, but it has never been found naturally — and the reason is simple: whenever matter encounters antimatter they annihilate each other. Antimatter mirrors ordinary matter, with the same characteristics, except that their charges are opposite. The upshot of all this is that, if at the beginning of the universe there had been equal amounts of matter and antimatter, they would have blasted each other into oblivion. In other words, it would have been a Big Bang — and nothing but a Big Bang.

For our universe to form there must have been a precise amount more matter than antimatter, so when they had finished blasting each other to smithereens, there was exactly enough matter left to form our cosmos. If there had been a bit too little matter then there would not have been enough to form the universe, and if there had been a dash too much, the fledgling cosmos would have collapsed in on itself. A variation of as slight as one particle per ten billion would have been enough to prevent our life-sustaining universe from coming into being. In terms of a cosmic game of roulette — the odds were obscenely stacked against us existing. But amazingly, it was exactly right. Paul Davies, Professor of Natural Philosophy at the University of Adelaide, likens this precision to 'aiming at a target an inch wide on the other side of the observable universe and hitting the mark'.[5] And as Timothy Ferris, Berkeley professor and popular science writer adds, we would have no more expected this to have arisen by chance 'than a pole vaulter's pole to remain standing, poised on its tip, for centuries following his vault'.[6]

But the lottery for life is even more unlikely than that. The atheist astronomer Sir Fred Hoyle discovered how carbon and oxygen were created in the fiery interior of stars. 'It just happens' that this feat depends critically on what is called the internal resonance of the nuclei of the oxygen and carbon atoms. This led Astronomer Royal Sir Martin Rees and science writer

John Gribbin, who, incidentally, do not believe in God, to state, 'This combination of coincidences ... is indeed remarkable. There is no better evidence to support the argument that the universe has been designed for our benefit — tailor-made for man.'[7] Fred Hoyle confessed, 'Nothing has shaken my atheism as much as this discovery.'[8]

When all this is put together, it seems that a great deal of incredibly unlikely coincidences have had to happen in order to allow our universe to exist at all — and another set of unbelievable accidents have had to occur for life to be viable. The real question is this: How many coincidences are needed before they can't be seen as coincidences?

As we look closely at the burrow of cause and effect, it is strange how everything on planet earth is 'just right' to allow life to exist — or indeed, anything to exist. Is this luck, or is it deliberate design?

Surely the Hat Would Have Killed the Rabbit

If the rabbit (life) was pulled out of the hat (the universe) this is particularly strange and unaccountable when the general conditions of the universe are utterly hostile to life. The hat would have killed the rabbit.

Our universe is very sterile — it's a dangerous place to live. Stars have temperatures of millions of degrees centigrade and issue radiation with unimaginable destructive force. There are places where gravity is so strong that hydrogen gas is turned into a silver solid, and other places where the gravitational pull is so enormous that not even light can escape — the mysterious black holes. And then there is an unfathomable immensity of apparent nothingness — with temperatures below anything we can conceive. Space is utterly inhospitable — except for one known exception. The planet earth is unique.

Stephen Hawking, professor at Cambridge University, has called our planet 'a medium-sized planet orbiting around an average star in the outer suburbs of an ordinary spiral galaxy'.[9] And yet, this planet is special. Astronaut Guy Gardner, who has seen the earth from the perspective of the moon, points out that, 'the more we learn and see about our universe the more we come to realise that the most ideally suited place for life within the entire solar system is the planet we call home.'[10]

If our planet is an unlikely exception to a momentously destructive universe, then the fact that life exists here at all is even more inconceivable. The crude, raw forces of nature do not naturally lead to such a harmonious, intricate, delicate, ordered, and stunningly complex thing as what we blandly call 'life'.

How come we live on such a finely balanced, intricately complicated world, which has life — and more than that, sustains life? Our planet protects us from the destructive forces of space and cocoons us in an environment that has just the right temperature, just the right atmosphere, just the right sunlight and just the right gravity to enable profoundly beautiful and complex life forms to flourish. And this is seen to be the result of an explosion, the Big Bang. Explosions are not known for bringing order and beauty. It seems that there has to be more to the universe than just the universe. It can't explain itself.

UFO Sightings

For many, the whole thing is just too improbable to be brought about by chance — there must be some rhyme or reason to it all. However, instead of taking their thoughts to where they could logically lead (an infinite Creator) they stutter to a halt once they reach what we call 'space'. Here they cast around for something extraordinary, mysterious and intelligent to give a personal dimension to what they otherwise consider an unbearably impersonal and inexplicable universe. Bizarrely, instead of

an ultimate being, they lower their gaze and look for something smaller — they seek for aliens. As Carl Sagan put it, perhaps overzealously, 'The search for life elsewhere is something that which runs so deep in human curiosity that there is not a human being anywhere in the world who isn't interested in the question.'[11]

The hopeful hunt for extraterrestrial beings at least gives the suggestion of personality in the cosmos. Those unable to cope with an impersonal universe feel there must be some kind of intelligent life out there. In essence, and perhaps surprisingly for many, this is essentially a religious search — deep down we want to make contact with an intelligence greater than ourselves. We desire to connect with a being superior to ourselves — secretly and even unconsciously we desire to worship. For many millennia this less than fully conscious search has taken us through a belief in gods, ghosts, spirits, angels, demons and the supernatural in general. There seems to be a 'God-shaped hole' buried within our consciousness, and even if we turn away from an ultimate being, we still attempt to satiate our thirst with something lesser — hence the hunt for UFOs. It is as spiritual as it is scientific.

Over the years there have been many claims of UFO sightings. A few more recent ones include those in China, Germany and Montenegro. In 2002, four UFOs were spotted flying over Beijing — they were flying at a height of 10 kilometres and moving in pairs. The Shanghai Star quoted the Beijing Times as saying they appeared for around an hour. Lan Songzhu of Xinglong Observation Station of Beijing Astronomical Observatory said that there have been more than 10,000 recorded UFO sightings in the last hundred years. He believed that about ninety-five percent of these sightings have been shown to be related to the global magnetic field, astronomy, or the atmosphere.

Early in 2002, hundreds of people reported seeing mysterious UFOs over southern Germany. The Bavarian interior minister said that hundreds of worried citizens called to report the

UFOs, describing a loud explosion, a series of flashes and other strange lights in the sky. Germany's national weather service says it is possible a meteor or a piece of space junk burned up or exploded as it entered the earth's atmosphere.

There have also been other UFO sightings in the last few years — hundreds of people in a Montenegrin village reported hearing a series of loud blasts and saw massive illuminated objects hovering overhead. According to the newspaper Vijesti, many witnesses claimed the UFOs changed shape before heading off into the sky and out of sight.

Interest in UFOs and aliens has reached epidemic proportions — sightings and abductions being recorded all the time. In fact, UFO researcher Ann Druffel has published a book on how to fend off alien attack. Her book, *How to Defend Yourself Against Alien Abductions*, gives step-by-step instructions on what to do if you find yourself the target of extra-terrestrial intrusion.

When the humorous travel writer Bill Bryson packed his bags in England and returned to his native USA, he says he did so because his countrymen needed him — he had read that 3.7 million Americans believed they had been abducted by aliens at one time or another.

The questions, 'Are we alone in the universe?' and 'Is there intelligent life out there?' have always aroused interest. Around the world there are various SETI (Search for Extraterrestrial Intelligence) programmes that are part of the ongoing scientific research effort aimed at detecting radio signals from extraterrestrial civilizations. These research bodies use many observatories such as the one at Arecibo, which has recently logged a total of 10,000 hours of observation time; they also gather information from satellites.

Recent advances in technology make laser pulses a viable means of communicating over vast distances. If intelligent alien lifeforms are using similar technology, these research projects will be able to detect them.

The important question to ask those who run the SETI projects is: 'How would you know that a signal from outer space was caused by intelligent life?' One of their key answers is that if a signal were produced by extraterrestrial intelligence, it would have a pattern to it; there would be something about it, which was not random.

The interesting thing about this is that while they star-gaze there is just such a pattern already here beneath our noses. If we turn the telescope downwards and we look through the microscope, what do we see? Even in the simplest cells we find far more than a crude pattern, but organization, and more than that, we find complex information. In the nuclei of cells there is a code and a mechanism for decoding its messages, so that the hidden information is employed in building and sustaining living organisms. This is information technology far more sophisticated than human intelligence and ingenuity have produced. In the simplest cell we have information equivalent to a hundred million pages of the *Encyclopaedia Britannica* — surely that can't have happened by random chemical motion.

The tapestry of life begins with a single thread. Through the most amazing precision, a microscopic egg in one human being is fertilized by a sperm cell from another — and this resultant fertilized egg, the size of a pinhead, contains chemical instructions that would fill more than 500,000 printed pages. In time the fertilized egg divides into the 30 trillion cells that make up the human body, including 12 billion brain cells, which form more than 120 trillion connections. This cell contains all the information to shape a growing human being, with every curve of their body, the colour of their eyes, the shade of their hair, the expression of their smile and the sparkle in their eyes. In the face of such a miracle we can but stand in silent awe.

When the sperm entered the egg and produced the first cell which became you, the reader of this book, all the information needed was present. All the different types of cells, tissues and organs were encoded, as were the physical qualities, which make you look like you. This, along with the information processing needed to turn that chemical 'potential you' in a bit of DNA into the 'actual you' today, is utterly staggering.

This raises a profound question: if a pattern in radio-waves from outer-space could be construed as being caused by intelligent beings, why then is it that the infinitely more complex language system of DNA is explained away as the result of random processes? Surely the intricate patterns, processes and information technology of our cells bare eloquent testimony to an intelligent Creator.

A Stroll around Lilliput

The life-forms of planet earth certainly appear to be designed — after all, could raw, blind and random chance throw up something so intricate? The language of DNA, when spoken by the nucleus of cells, makes molecules called amino acids. These basic building blocks of life, when arranged specifically and precisely, are built into bigger molecules called proteins. Proteins make life happen. Life is ultimately a molecular phenomenon. All organisms are made of molecules that act as the nuts and bolts and gears and pulleys of biological systems. The processes, interactions, control systems of this miniscule world are staggeringly complex, all the way from the tiniest bacterium through to the cells making up the reader and writer of this page. But how can we explain this Lilliputian world that allows, controls and causes all our movements and interactions? Michael Behe, Professor of Biochemistry at Lehigh University writes: 'Vision, motion, and other biological functions have proven to be no less sophisticated than television cameras and automobiles. Science has made enormous progress in understanding how the chemistry of life works, but the elegancy and complexity of biological systems at the molecular level have paralysed science's attempt to account for the origin of specific, complex biomolecular systems.'[12]

Professor Behe draws the conclusion that only design can explain the biochemical world that is all around and within us. His words are so powerful here that they are worth quoting in full:

Over the past four decades modern biochemistry has uncovered the secrets of the cell. The progress has been hard won. It has required tens of thousands of people to dedicate the better part of their lives to the tedious work of the laboratory. Graduate students in untied tennis shoes scraping around in the lab late on Saturday night; postdoctoral associates working fourteen hours a day seven days a week; professors ignoring their children in order to polish and repolish grant proposals, hoping to shake a little money loose from politicians with larger constituencies to feed — these are the people that make scientific research move forward. The knowledge we now have of life at the molecular level has been stitched together from innumerable experiments in which proteins were purified, genes cloned, electron micrographs taken, cells cultured, structures determined, sequences compared, parameters varied, and controls done. Papers were published, results checked, reviews written, blind alleys searched, and new leads fleshed out.

The result of these cumulative efforts to investigate the cell — to investigate life at the molecular level - is a loud, clear, piercing cry of 'design!' The result is so unambiguous and so significant that it must be ranked as one of the greatest achievements in the history of science. The discovery rivals those of Newton and Einstein, Lavoisier and Schödinger, Pasteur, and Darwin. The observation of the intelligent design of life is as momentous as the observation that the earth goes around the sun or that disease is caused by bacteria or that radiation is emitted in quanta. The magnitude of the victory, gained at such a great cost through sustained effort over the course of decades, would be expected to send cham-

pagne corks flying in labs around the world. This triumph of science should evoke cries of 'Eureka!' from ten thousand throats, should occasion much hand-slapping and high-fiving, and perhaps even be an excuse to take a day off.

But no bottles have been uncorked, no hands slapped. Instead, a curious, embarrassed silence surrounds the star complexity of the cell. When the subject comes up in public, feet start to shuffle, and breathing gets a bit laboured. In private people are a bit more relaxed; many explicitly admit the obvious but then stare at the ground, shake their heads, and let it go at that.

Why does the scientific community not greedily embrace this startling discovery? Why is the observation of design handled with intellectual gloves? The dilemma is that while one side of the elephant is labelled 'design', the other side might be labelled 'God'. [13]

The White Rabbit's burrow didn't dig itself — it was dug — and meticulously dug at that.

"'Curiouser and curiouser" cried Alice

(she was so much surprised, that for the moment she quite forgot how to speak good English).'

All this seems most curious. It is curious that the universe is here at all; it is curious that life is here; it is curious that we are here. What we daily pass off as ordinary is in reality most extraordinary. The more we peer down the burrow the stranger it all becomes.

And then, why does it all hold together so neatly? Why are the laws of the universe so precise and predictable? Nothing about what we perceive as ordinary is really 'ordinary' at all — it is commonplace, yes, but when we look more closely, what we pass by as 'ordinary' is actually extraordinary, in the sense that it is amazing. None of this can surely be explained by chance. Would it not be better to suppose that behind it all is a being that created it, including all its laws, and that this being also maintains and upholds it all?

If this is the case, then in a very real sense there is something supernatural behind the natural. And if this is true, he could occasionally alter or suspend his own laws and patterns of normal operation. These would be rare events, which we would call 'miracles', and would be consistent with this conception of the universe and what is behind it. If this being wanted to get our attention and cause us to stop and listen he could well do it this way.

Deeper and Deeper

"'Well!' thought Alice, to herself, "after such a fall as this, I shall think nothing of tumbling down the stairs."'

As we explore the 'burrow' of the universe we are led to entertain the possibility that there is something, or someone, behind it. If this is so, and if for a moment we suppose that this is a 'someone' rather than a 'something', that is, a personal being, it seems perfectly conceivable that 'he' might want to make himself known to us. If this creator-God made and sustains the whole universe, would he remain silent?

*Into the doubt and confusion of our guesswork and hunches,
God has spoken.*

The Voice

The White Rabbit and his amazing burrow lead us to suspect an alternative understanding of reality than that which is commonly held today. They suggest the existence of some supreme being — a being which could perhaps be labelled 'God'.

There is a problem though, and a big one at that: although the universe seems to point us to the concept of God, it does so without giving any content to that word. We may suspect that there is some kind of ultimate being out there, but from what we have looked at so far, we do not know much about him, nor can he make any difference in our lives. What we are left with is a massive question mark. The Big Question we looked at, at the beginning, needs expanding: it is not only a question as to whether some sort of God exists, but what that God is like — and more than that, what he demands from us and wishes to give to us. If our concept of 'God' is merely a religious black hole, a cosmic blank space — if the word 'God' has no real meaning — then it is pointless asking whether he exists. The Big Question, therefore, must grow bigger.

The trouble is that our suspicions are aroused, but we don't know exactly what, or who, to suspect with regards to God. We have no detail. The stage is set, the music starts, the lights come on — and we wait with bated breath. The curtain now needs to be pulled back to reveal what is beyond. So far, it is rather like we have found a runway in a jungle — but now we wait in expectation for what will arrive. Runways indicate planes, but tell us little about them. The universe points to God's existence, but it does not tell us much about him.

If this God has taken so much care to bring into being creatures like ourselves, surely it is not inconceivable that he would

want to reveal more of himself to us. Having aroused our curiosity with tantalizing clues that seem to indicate his existence, it would seem reasonable to expect him to satisfy that curiosity.

If we are to know what God is like and what he expects from us, it has to be revealed to us. God has to reveal himself — he has to speak. We are limited beings and we have limited information, and so, by definition, we cannot investigate that which is infinite. If we are to know anything more than God's mere existence, it has to be communicated to us. It is not enough for God simply to be there; he has to supernaturally speak in order for us to understand anything about him. We need to receive speech, that is, words, or language, about this ultimate being and from this ultimate being.

Suspicious Software

There is something about human beings that can make us very suspicious — our mental software seems to be designed, and designed to understand communication. We are beings that understand speech — language comes naturally to us. It seems that we are programmed to handle language. The hardware of our bodies — ears and voice box — and the software of our minds appears to be specifically designed to recognize, learn, think and communicate in words.

But what is particularly fascinating is that our language — what we think and what we say — correlates with the external physical world. The software of our minds is compatible with the hard realities of time and space and the laws that govern it. The more we explore and discover with our science, the more we find that our language can describe it, our language can communicate it and our language can be used to predict what will happen based on what we have discovered and described. In other words, there is more to language than just what is inside our heads: it works when applied to the external world. So, the language in my head works when it communicates ideas to your head (if you follow!), and it is efficient at describing and explaining the external world. In other words, whatever the postmodernists might say, to an extremely large extent, language works.[1]

Language not only correlates effectively with the world outside of our heads, it also is inherently built on a logical framework internally. Even children argue and are concerned about truth. But why is this? More than that, they don't need to be trained to argue and show errors and inconsistencies in an opponent's perspective. Why is this? Could this have happened by chance?

If I am nothing more than a sophisticated ape, blindly evolved from some primeval soup by the random interaction of atoms, how can I trust my reasoning to be logical? If my brain is the result of a cosmic lottery, why should its thought processes be rational? That is surely a step of blind faith.

Yet atheists always assume they have the intellectual high ground — they give the impression they are the logical ones, whereas Christians are those who have taken the fanciful leap of faith. One of Britain's most distinguished writers and broadcasters, Sir Ludovic Kennedy, wrote a book, *All in the mind: A farewell to God*, in which he said he wanted 'definitively to disprove the existence of God'.[2] But to 'disprove' the existence of God he makes a massive assumption — that we have minds capable of proving or disproving something. How can he make such an assumption when he believes the universe is the product of random processes?

The biologist (and atheist) J. B. S. Haldane once wrote, 'If my mental processes are determined wholly by the motions in my brain, I have no reason to suppose that my beliefs are true.'[3] Professor C. S. Lewis put the same point most eloquently when he said,

> *If the solar system was brought about by an accidental collision, then the appearance of organic life on this planet was*

also an accident, and the whole evolution of man was an accident too. If so, then all our present thoughts are mere accidents — the accidental by-product of the movement of atoms ... Why should we believe them to be true? I see no reason for believing that one accident should be able to give me a correct account of all the other accidents. It's like expecting that the accidental shape taken by the splash when you upset a milk jug should give you a correct account of how the jug was made and why it was upset.[4]

Even Charles Darwin put it this way: 'The horrid doubt always arises whether the convictions of a man's mind, which has developed from the mind of the lower animals, are of any value or at all trustworthy.'[5]

In other words, the atheist has pulled the logical rug from under his own feet. For him to be right, he has to think rationally. But, his own theory does not allow any thought to be rational. Why should his brain be intelligent and sensible when it was formed out of unintelligent matter and by random chance? It is an illogical leap to say that the raw, undirected elements of the universe can produce reasoning minds. Surely those who believe in a creator-God are on more solid ground. Human beings are designed — and designed to think. This is a far better explanation of the way things really are. So when a Christian gives a reason for what he believes, he does so on the basis that reason really exists — and that he and his hearers can comprehend that reason.[6]

Pulling all this together, there seems to be something very suspicious here: against all odds, we homo sapiens are built with the complex mental software to use and understand language. Furthermore, this internal mental language system actually works in describing and communicating our understanding of the external world — we can talk to each other about what we see and experience. On top of this, our internal psychological software, our physical hardware and the laws of the universe all correlate and are compatible with each other. The logic of the laws of the universe can be understood by the inherent logic of our minds — they appear to have one Designer. And then, alongside all this, our minds seem to be programmed to be capable to think logically. In short, we can describe what we see, we can think about it and we can talk about it. Surely the best way of explaining all this is to assume that it was all designed by one mind and created by one being — God.

Now, if this God made my mind, your mind, the physical universe and our linguistic capacity to communicate what we comprehend, then it is quite coherent to suppose that if this God wished to reveal more of himself to us, he would use language. After all, he made it.

Message in a Bottle

More than this, we could quite reasonably suppose that such a revelation would be a written one. If it were not, God would have to the say the same thing over and over again to almost every individual through every period of history — misunderstanding and misinterpretation would be rife. However, if God were to communicate to mankind and then get that revelation fixed in written form, it would become a permanent record. If God spoke through a variety of means to a variety of special people and then enabled all this to be brought together into one volume, humanity would have a permanent message from its Maker. This fixed message could then be looked at and examined; it could be validated and confirmed; it could be explored and understood. In essence, it would be a means of communicating accurately through time and space. Whether read in A.D. 500, or A.D. 1250, or A.D. 2006, the message could be understood; it is not bound by time. More than that, whatever the culture or geographical region, its meaning could be grasped; it is not bound by space. And, most amazingly, built into the

concept and reality of communication through language is the beautifully practical idea of translation. Whether the recipients speak ancient Greek, or Middle English, Icelandic, or whatever, its words, sentences and meaning can be accurately translated. Here is a supernatural message bobbing on the sea of human society and thought, unbound by time and space —wherever it goes it can be picked up and read.

The Bible claims to be that supernatural language-based revelation to us. Again and again throughout its pages it claims to be just that, the written message of God. In the Old Testament the phrase 'Thus says the Lord' appears hundreds of times.[7] Furthermore, God is often said to speak 'through' the prophets.[8] The Old Testament prophets knew that the Spirit of God governed what they said. For example, one of them put it like this: 'I am filled with power, with the Spirit of the Lord.'[9] And another states, 'The Spirit of the Lord spoke through me; his word was on my tongue.'[10]

The New Testament writers also claimed to speak and write with the authority of God. One puts it in this way: 'We speak, not in words taught by human reason but in words taught by the Spirit, expressing spiritual truths in spiritual words.'[11] Another passage expresses the Bible's radical claim in these words: 'All Scripture is inspired by God and is profitable for teaching, rebuking, correcting and training in righteousness.'[12]

The Bible claims nothing less for itself than to be the written Word of God.

That's All Very Well…

It's all very well for the Bible to claim for itself to be God's supernatural revelation to us, but that claim has to be justified in some way. We live in a world where many claims are made about many things — and many are utterly false. More than that, most religions have their special books that they claim have supernatural wisdom. So what is so special about the Bible? Why should this book be taken any more seriously than any other book that claims to have divine origin? Why should we give its apparently absurd and outdated claim to be God's special message to us a second thought?

Again and again throughout the generations, readers have found that through reading the Bible's pages they have had the profound sense that something strangely supernatural was going on — the God behind the universe was communicating with them. This effect has been so amazing that some of these people have turned the world upside down. The Bible has an inherent power of its own, which people experience. When people read it, many testify to hearing God speak through its pages, having their lives revolutionized and discovering new meaning, peace and purpose to their existence.

No book has influenced so many individuals or affected so many societies as the Bible. Cleland McAfee writes in *The Greatest English Classic*: 'If every Bible in any considerable city were destroyed, the Bible could be restored in all its essential parts from the quotations on the shelves of the city public library. There are works, covering almost all the great literary writers, devoted especially to showing how much the Bible has influenced them.'[13] This is just the sort of unique effect we would expect from a book in which God was speaking to us.

This unique book has shaped much of our society's landscape for good. Those whose minds were enflamed by the Bible changed society — they fought against the slave trade, set up hospitals, founded schools, established orphanages and worked for religious liberty. Without the Bible, this world would be a poorer and more tragic place.

The Bible has been read by more people and published in more languages than any other publication — indeed, it has been the most persecuted book in history. More copies have been produced of the whole Bible and more extracts and selections than of any other book. The Bible's claim to be God's

message to humanity is reinforced by the unique effect it has had on individuals, communities and societies.

All this by itself doesn't prove the Bible to be God speaking, but it does show it to be a very special, unique book. Such a book cannot be discounted out of hand, as many do with it today — it deserves thoughtful attention from any serious enquirer after truth.

Seeing into the Future

What would make someone really start to wonder whether this book has something supernatural about it? Perhaps the answer might be if it could be shown that it has successfully predicted some future events hundreds of years in advance. For many that would be conclusive. None of us can travel in time, and although we might be able to deduce some future events a little in advance with a few calculated guesses, anything more than this is impossible. If this book does make accurate predictions, or prophecies, that have been clearly fulfilled, then something very peculiar is going on indeed.

One of the most remarkable credentials of the Bible is that it can be shown again and again to have accurately predicted the future. Only God knows what will happen in the future and if this is predicted accurately and precisely then it shows that the message comes from him.

This accurate prediction is actually a test the Bible itself gives for discovering whether God is speaking, or a fraudster. The Old Testament puts it in this way: 'You may say to yourselves, "How can we know when a message has not been spoken by the Lord?" If what a prophet proclaims in the name of the Lord does not take place or come true, that is a message the Lord has not spoken.'[14]

One example of the Bible's many prophecies is where it predicts, hundreds of years before the event that the Messiah would be born in Bethlehem.[15] The prophecy says, 'But you, Bethlehem Ephrathah, though you are small among the clans of Judah, out of you will come for me one who will be ruler over Israel, whose origins are of old, from ancient times.' And then, years later we read in the New Testament the history of where Jesus was born in Bethlehem.[16]

Other predictions include that the coming Messiah will be a son of David,[17] that he will work in the area known as Galilee,[18] be killed by being pierced,[19] die a criminal's death[20] and yet come back to life again.[21] With regards to Jesus' betrayal, the Old Testament amazingly prophesies startling details, including his actual betrayal by a close friend,[22] for thirty pieces of silver,[23] that this money would be thrown into God's house[24] and the money used to buy a potter's field.[25] These are just a few, by way of illustration — there are too many to consider them fully.

Some have objected to this by saying that Jesus intentionally made his life fit the prophecies. But although this allegation might seem to be possible for a few of the prophecies, many concern events Jesus could never have arranged, including his ancestry, how he was betrayed for a specific amount of money, how he was put to death, the fact that his bones remained unbroken and that soldiers cast lots for his clothing.

Another objection is that it is possible that several people in history have fitted these predictions, and that Jesus happened to have a better spin-doctor, so he is the one everyone remembers. However, the probability of this occurring is so unlikely that for all practical purposes it is impossible. For example, to take but a few of the prophecies into account, that person would have to be a Jew, from the tribe of Judah, from the family line of Jesse, and from the royal line of King David, who was born in Bethlehem. That eliminates most people in the world. Then he would have to be betrayed by a friend, sold for thirty pieces of silver, have his hands and feet pierced, be executed with thieves and buried in a rich man's tomb. How many people in history fit

all these criteria — and there are many more precise prophecies than this.

Some people have tried to explain these prophecies away by saying that they were written at or after the times they purported to describe. In other words, they were a political or religious comment at that time rather than prediction. This is easily answered, as most scholars would estimate that the original documents were written at least 400 years prior to the events predicted, and even if that is not believed, we have a Greek translation of the Old Testament that was translated about 200 B.C.

The Bible's accurate prophecies that are precisely fulfilled reinforce the belief that this book is perhaps God's special written message to humanity.

Elaborate Fairytales?

Some sceptical readers might interject at this point and say that they have already dismissed the Bible as nothing more than an elaborate fairytale. Sure, fact may be buried there somewhere, but it has been buried under so many layers of fiction and myth that only a mere trace of the truth is at all discernable. Of course, it has to be recognized that if the Bible is just a string of fairytales then a very big question arises on the basis of what we have just looked at: why should fairytales be able to predict the future? This makes them pretty peculiar fairytales, indeed, it shows they are not fictional. But this is not the only reason for dismissing the fairytale option.

Again and again the Bible has been shown to be an accurate historical record. Even after over two centuries of sustained attack by liberal academics, who have tried to show it to be little more than a myth, the Bible has continually managed to reassert itself. Whether we look at the archaeological evidence, the scientific data, the number of early manuscripts, or the criteria for analyzing the accuracy and reliability of our present documents, the Bible shows itself to be correct again and again. Whichever way we look at the evidence, the Bible is believable.[26]

In every instance where we can test the Bible we find that it is factually accurate, even down to fine details. This being so, it is not a step of blind faith to trust the writers where we cannot test them. Therefore it is quite reasonable to accept its testimony with regards to miracles.

What is more, the human authors of the various parts of Scripture demonstrate the most profound sense of personal morality and honesty — they wrote what they believed to be the case. These human writers never hid the failings of the various characters and heroes of the text. Once these points are put together we can see that it is utterly amazing what the Bible actually communicates in terms of the supernatural. The Bible does not shrink back from recording miracles.

Cosmic Rule-breaking

Some people dismiss the Bible out of hand because it contains miracles, without realizing that such a prejudiced opinion is based upon a supposition of blind faith that miracles are impossible. David Hume, the avowed anti-Christian philosopher, was so dogmatic about this that he refused even to consider possible evidence of such occurrences. This can hardly be the attitude of a seeker after truth. To deny evidence simply because it points to something we have not experienced is to be biased in the extreme.

The basic issue at stake is whether we will accept the supernatural at all. If there really is a God, then logically he may suspend any law of nature if he chooses to do so. And if Jesus was truly God, this power must have been extended to him as well. The belief that miracles cannot happen presupposes that we live in a universe that is a closed system of rules of cause and effect that cannot be broken. But as we saw earlier, the very existence

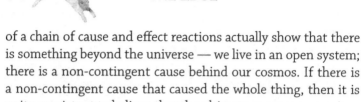

of a chain of cause and effect reactions actually show that there is something beyond the universe — we live in an open system; there is a non-contingent cause behind our cosmos. If there is a non-contingent cause that caused the whole thing, then it is quite consistent to believe that the ultimate cause can occasionally change or supersede those chains of cause and effect we see around us. We live in an open system — miracles are therefore possible.

This is not to say that we would see the laws of nature broken all the time — that would lead to chaos. The point of the laws of nature is that generally and normally they are laws, and so are rarely broken. But theoretically the possibility exists. This is exactly what we see in the Bible. We don't see miracles all over the place, but we do see them. And generally, when we see them they are grouped around special events. They are there for a specific purpose: to validate those events.

As we peruse the length and breadth of the Bible, we see that, in particular, miracles are grouped around the giving of the Law of God and the establishment of a very special people, who were going to show how a relationship with God works out in practice. And then we see another cluster at a crisis point in Israel's history when they were being called back from rebellion and sin to serve the Lord again in accordance with that divine revelation given earlier. But the greatest cluster of miracles surrounds and are performed by the Lord Jesus Christ. Jesus Christ is God's clearest revelation of himself to us. In a very real sense, he is the pivotal point of reference for all communication and language in the universe: he is the Word of God. It is that Word that we must now listen to.

In the beginning was the Word, and the Word was with God, and the Word was God. He was with God in the beginning.

Through him all things were made; without him nothing was made that has been made. In him was life, and that life was the light of men. The light shines in the darkness, but the darkness has not understood it.

He was in the world, and though the world was made through him, the world did not recognize him.

The Word became flesh and made his dwelling among us. We have seen his glory, the glory of the One and Only, who came from the Father, full of grace and truth.

The Bible
John 1:1-5, 10, 14

As we have followed the burrow of cause and effect we have seen that it leads inevitably to some ultimate uncaused being. Behind the contingent cosmos there has to be a non-contingent cause. This is consistent with a belief in God.

Furthermore, we have noted that the burrow, our universe, appears to be beautifully and wonderfully designed. The burrow must have had an architect. This also is consistent with a belief in God.

But the burrow also has writing on it; there are messages written on its walls. This ultimate being, who made the whole universe, us, and our ability to communicate in language, has revealed himself in a written message: the Bible.

Now, suppose, as we stand there pondering, looking at this writing on the walls of the burrow, that we realize that in the past someone has come up from the dark end of the tunnel and stepped into human history. Suppose that it suddenly becomes apparent that God has come out of his 'totally other' supernatural domain and actually entered ours; God has entered the burrow from the other end.

The Word became flesh and made his dwelling among us. We have seen his glory, the glory of the One and Only, who came from the Father, full of grace and truth.

John 1:14

The Word

What if the ultimate being came up the burrow to meet us?

That is exactly what God has done in Jesus Christ — he has broken into his creation to reveal himself. Imagine if this God came into our world — how would he come? How would we understand him? Surely, the best way would be for him to take human form.

We have examined the idea that God made the external laws of the universe totally compatible with the internal software of our minds. We can explore and think about the world around us. Furthermore, we can communicate that knowledge with each other. According to this proposition, both language and what language communicates were made by God; they correlate with each other. God's creation is understandable through language and that understanding can be communicated through language. Language, comprising of words, seems to be at the very core of things.

In one passage of the Bible Jesus Christ is called the Word of God.[1] Jesus is God's clearest and most supreme communication to us; he is God's message to us. Imagine if God wanted to clearly disclose himself to us, how would he do it? Surely, it would be quite coherent to suggest that in some way he would come into our world. After all, writing to someone is one thing; going and meeting them is another. By entering into our world and taking on our humanity he would be able to reveal himself to us in a way far more clearly than through prophets or miracles. This is exactly what the Bible claims. One of Jesus' original followers put it like this: 'The Word became flesh and lived for a while among us. We have seen his glory, the glory of the one and only Son, who came from the Father, full of grace and truth.'[2]

Jesus — the Word of God

This is mind boggling in the extreme — that the Creator should step into his creation, that the eternal and timeless one should wrap himself in temporal flesh. The concepts here are quite staggering: the infinite Maker of everything contracts himself to a finite body. Our minds quite naturally reel and are confounded, if not confused. This is possibly the most profound thought and truth in the universe, and so it is not surprising that our finite minds struggle and intellectually wheeze and pant. The Bible puts it this way regarding Jesus Christ:

> *Who being in very nature God,*
> *did not consider equality with God*
> *something to be grasped,*
> *but made himself nothing,*
> *taking the very nature of a servant,*
> *being made in human likeness.[3]*

Now, if this Jesus was indeed God, we would expect him to be unique. And this is exactly what we find in the Bible. Whatever way we look at Jesus we can see that he is utterly unique — which is exactly what we would expect if he is God's anointed Messiah, or Christ — his messenger to humanity.

Unique Miracles

Jesus' miracles cannot be ignored — they are described in almost every strand of the gospels and even in Jewish writings as well. He made the lame walk, the dumb speak, the blind see, and even brought some dead people back to life. Nor was his power confined to the realm of healing; he also demonstrated his control over nature. He ordered water to become wine and fed a crowd of 5,000 from five little loaves of bread and two small fish.

The storm subsided and the tempestuous waves were stilled at his command.

A Unique Character

Jesus had a unique character, or personality. We could spend a long time looking at his poise, his majesty, his love, his humility, his thoughtfulness, and his devotion. Wherever he went he cared for the lonely, the sick, the social outcasts, and all in need. No one can fail to admire the beauty of his character, but there is one feature which makes him unique and that is his moral perfection. There was honesty and integrity about Jesus' life which meant that neither his closest friends nor his enemies could find any fault with him. Peter said that he was 'without blemish or defect'[4] and 'committed no sin',[5] and John said that Jesus is 'the righteous one'[6] 'and in him is no sin'.[7]

A Unique Teacher

The moment Jesus opened his mouth he showed incredible power as a teacher. Soldiers who were sent to arrest him fell back in amazement and returned empty-handed, saying, 'Nobody taught like this man.'

Jesus taught with his own authority, rather than quoting the philosophers and teachers who preceded him. This thirty-year-old carpenter was so devastatingly good as a teacher that he threatened the religious academic professionals of the day, and the jealousy aroused contributed to his ultimate arrest and execution. No revolution throughout history can be compared to that which has been produced by the words of Jesus. Without money and arms he has conquered more people than any emperor of history. He spoke such words as have never been spoken before or since and without writing a single line 'he set

more pens in motion and furnished themes for more sermons, orations, discussions, learned volumes, works of art and songs of praise than the whole army of great men of ancient and modern times'.

Jesus spoke with such originality and had such profound insight that, even in the estimation of those who have no belief in his claims, he is respected as being in the first rank of those of genius and probably the greatest moral reformer and martyr who has ever lived.

A Unique Effect on History

Jesus' effect on history indicates that his claims are true. Someone once wrote: 'He never wrote a book. He never held an office. He never had a family or owned a house. He didn't go to college. He never visited a big city. He never travelled more than 200 miles from the place where he was born. He did none of the things one usually associates with greatness. He had no credentials but himself . . . [Twenty] centuries have come and gone and today he is the central figure of the human race. All the armies that ever marched, all the navies that ever sailed, all the parliaments that ever sat, all the kings that ever reigned, put together, have not affected the life of man on earth as much as that one solitary life!'

Even the atheist author and historian H. G. Wells has made this admission, as if, in spite of himself, he must recognize something about Christ: 'I am a historian, I am not a believer. But this penniless preacher from Galilee is irresistibly the centre of history.'

A Unique Effect on Lives

The original disciples were utterly transformed by their belief in the resurrection of Jesus Christ. They were transformed from normal folk like mere artisans and tradesmen in an obscure corner of the Roman Empire into a body of people who totally revolutionized the world. These men, who claimed to have seen the risen Christ, suffered for their beliefs — and some died for them. From the courage, devotion and energy of these men, a whole culture was overthrown and the world's largest religion was established.

And this power of the risen Jesus to change lives was passed on — throughout the last 2,000 years, millions of people have had their lives revolutionized. They have fed the poor, cared for the sick, established schools, fought for justice and been the greatest force for good this world has ever seen.

A Unique Resurrection

Millions upon millions of Christians throughout the last 2,000 years have believed that Jesus came back to life after being executed by the Roman authorities. More than that, they believe he is still alive today. And this is not the mere fairy-tale fantasy of deluded simpletons — many learned researchers, scholars and lawyers have had a hard look at the evidence and have concluded that these claims are true.

For example, Sir Edward Clarke, K. C., wrote, 'As a lawyer I have made a prolonged study of the evidences for the events of the first Easter Day. To me the evidence is conclusive, and over and over again in the High Court I have secured a verdict on evidence not nearly so compelling.' And then there is J. N. D. Anderson, former lawyer and professor of oriental law at the University of London, who wrote: 'The most drastic way of dismissing the evidence would be to say that these stories were mere fabrications, that they were pure lies. But as far as I know, not a single critic today would take such an attitude. In fact, it really would be an impossible position. Think of the number of witnesses, over 500. Think of the character of the witnesses, men and women who gave the world the highest ethical teaching it has ever known, and who even on the testimony of their enemies lived it out in their lives. Think of the psychological absurdity of picturing a little band of defeated cowards cowering in an upper room one day and a few days later being transformed into a company that no persecution could silence — and then attempting to attribute this dramatic change to nothing more convincing than a miserable fabrication they were trying to foist upon the world. That simply wouldn't make sense.'[8]

Stupendous Claims

Whatever way we look at Jesus, he is unique. And this unique-ness validates the stupendous claims he made for himself. Among other things he claimed to be the Messiah or Christ, God's special messenger, to forgive sins, to own the titles the 'Son of Man'[9] and the 'Son of God'[10] and to be the one who would conduct the final judgement. Taken together, these are a claim to be God!

Jesus' contemporaries were not in any doubt as to the strength of his claim: 'The Jews tried all the harder to kill him; not only was he breaking the Sabbath, but he was even calling God his own Father, making himself equal with God.'[11] When Jesus was being tried by the ruling Jewish authorities, the fol-lowing exchange took place:

'At daybreak the council of the elders of the people, both the chief priests and the teachers of the law, met together, and Jesus was led before them.

"If you are the Christ," they said, "tell us."

Jesus answered, "If I tell you, you will not believe me, and if I

*asked you, you would not answer. But from now on, the Son
of Man will be seated at the right hand of the mighty God."*

*They all asked, "Are you then the Son of God?" He said, "You
are right in saying I am."*

*Then they said, "Why do we need any more testimony? We
have heard it from his own lips.""*[12]

This Jesus is God revealing himself to us in the clearest possible way. Jesus Christ embodies God's message to humanity
— he is the living Word of God.[13] But what is more is that Jesus
adds his validation to the authority of the Bible. Jesus regarded
the Scriptures as the written Word of God, and an authoritative
revelation from God himself. He recognized the authority of the
Old Testament. Jesus saw the Old Testament as God speaking.[14]
Jesus also gave authority to the New Testament. He promised
that God would specially gift the apostles, so that they would be
able to remember all that he had said,[15] and that they would be
taught all spiritual truth.[16] Just before Jesus was taken up into
heaven, he gave these men a command.[17] They were commanded
to take his teaching to all nations, and he promised to help them
and subsequent believers in this task until he returned to earth.
Since the apostles would die, this commission could only be fulfilled in later generations by the message being written down. It
was the apostles who either wrote or oversaw the writing of the
books of the New Testament. Jesus gave authority to the Bible
being God's written Word to us.

God Has Spoken

When all this is put together we have an amazing result — the
only conclusion is that God has supernaturally spoken through
the Bible. Whatever way we look at it, the evidence is remarkable.

First, the Bible claims to be the Word of God. Second, many people have claimed to have experienced God speaking to them through it. Third, people have been so revolutionized by reading the Bible that they have had a unique and beneficial impact on the world. Fourth, this unique book contains prophecies that can be shown to have supernaturally predicted the future. Fifth, there are historically reliable accounts of miracles that verify the Bible's claims. Sixth, in particular, these miracles authenticate the claims of Jesus Christ to be God's special messenger. This Jesus is seen in a myriad of ways to be totally unique in the history of humanity — and this Jesus validates and confirms the Old and New Testaments to be God's written Word to us. God speaks to humanity through this unique book, the Bible.

But all this raises an even bigger issue — and that is, if God really has communicated to us, what in essence has he said? What is the essential message of this unique and supernatural book? What message does God want us to hear? What message did Jesus, the Word of God, bring to us? Nothing could be more important.

The Big Question grows even bigger.

It is not just that the burrow of the universe leads somewhere, to someone, but that that someone comes up the burrow to communicate to us.

The message must be vital.

The Message

We have followed the White Rabbit of cause and effect down his burrow and have ended up facing the reality of an Uncaused Cause. More than that, we have seen that the burrow shows such intricate complexity that it is impossible for it to have been 'dug' by chance — it was designed and built. This Uncaused Cause is also a Cosmic Designer. When all this is put together, we can say that it indicates some being of eternal power and divine nature[1]— a being we might well call 'God'.

We have also seen that this God has revealed himself clearly to us in the Bible and in Jesus Christ. God has spoken — his voice can be heard in the pages of Scripture. The Big Question now is what has he said? What is God's message to the world?

This is all part of the original Big Question, which as we have progressed, has enlarged. If God does exist, the focus of the question shifts to whether he has spoken, for if he hasn't then the whole thing is merely an academic mind game of no practical importance. But as we have discovered that God has spoken, then the focus of the Big Question shifts once again, and this time we ask what he has said. Nothing could be more important than this. What is the essence of this vital and supernatural message that is contained within the pages of the Bible, which all humanity needs to hear?

It is at a point like this that we often ask, 'Do you want the good news or the bad news?' The message from God contains both — the bad news is incredibly bad, and the good news is incredibly good. We will start with the bad news.

The Bad News

At the beginning of history God created a world that was good. He made it for men and women to enjoy and rule over; they were to be governors of his kingdom. To ensure that they owed their allegiance to him and that they did not grasp ultimate power for themselves, God gave them one restriction: they must not eat the fruit of a particular tree.[2] This tree was what he called 'the tree of the knowledge of good and evil'. It was not that the tree was some sort of magic, but it stood as a moral test. In eating from it they moved from obedience to disobedience.

The consequences of this action were immense and far beyond what the first man and woman could anticipate: they became frightened of their Maker, divided from each other and became ashamed of themselves.[3] More than this, their relationship with the physical world was suddenly precipitated into one of difficulty rather than unmitigated pleasure, resulting ultimately in a new and awful phenomenon: death. Alienation, suffering and death had entered the world.[4]

A bad life!

Throughout history, humanity has continued to confirm and reinforce this choice. People strangle their consciences and would rather worship anything other than their Lord and Maker. It is tragic to see how this works itself out in our lives and society. The Bible expresses the working out of this ongoing tragedy in the following words:

> *The wrath of God is being revealed from heaven against all the godlessness and wickedness of men who suppress the truth by their wickedness, since what may be known about God is plain to them. For since the beginning of the world God's invisible qualities — his eternal power and divine na-*

ture — *have been clearly seen, being understood from what has been made, so that men are without excuse.*

For although they knew God, they neither glorified him as God nor gave thanks to him, but their thinking became futile and their foolish hearts were darkened. Although they claimed to be wise, they became fools and exchanged the glory of the immortal God for images made to look like mortal man and birds and animals and reptiles.

Therefore God gave them over in the sexual desires of their hearts to sexual immorality for the degrading of their bodies with one another.[5]

This analysis shows how our rebellion from God has affected our thinking, our religion and our actions.

Our thinking becomes darkened

God made us rational beings capable of thinking; this is one of the aspects in which we are created in his image. What is not often clearly recognized today is that there is a link between our thinking and our morality. Our ability to think is part of who we are, it is not a separate entity. If we have turned from God and live in a way that is contrary to his standards, this will corrupt our thinking processes. Our deep and hidden motives — let alone our more open ones — will affect the way in which we reason.

Our religion becomes futile

One area of thinking which becomes particularly dark and confused concerns our relationship to God. Since we are created, we are of necessity dependent on our Creator. Even if we live as if he were not there, we cannot extinguish our need for him. Although we like to think we are independent and autonomous, in reality we are not. Deep down in our beings we have a desire to be dependent. The expression of our dependence is a form of worship and as such is religious. In our very natures we are religious beings that need and even crave to worship.

This deep and often unconscious craving to worship will surface, even in those who profess not to be religious. Today people are increasingly turning again to pagan deities, but the majority engage in more subtle forms of pseudo-religious worship. Some seek after the latest psychological guru or therapy technique and effectively begin worshipping themselves, desiring self-fulfilment, self-actualization, self-realization or enhanced self-esteem, depending on how the latest jargon expresses it. Others turn in a New Age direction, which takes this self-worship trend further by actually stating that we are gods.[6] Those not 'into this sort of thing' subconsciously worship themselves by allowing ambition, greed or pleasure to rule their lives. But whatever the particular manifestation of our pseudo-religious quest, we will not turn to the true God and worship him.

Our actions become wicked

When God is pushed out of the picture, we lose our basis for knowing what is right and what is wrong; once we lose the lawgiver there is no basis for law. Morality is all at sea. Even if we do think something is wrong, why should we bother to restrain ourselves? After all, if there is no judge or judgement, we may as well do whatever gives us pleasure and enjoyment, for we will never be held to account. As a result of turning from God, the basis for restraint disintegrates and the apparent freedom that we gain can only result in doing what is wrong. We have all broken the commands of God given in the Bible.[7]

One writer has put this in these words: 'With his vast scientific and technological know-how, man can break out of the earth's gravity and reach the moon, yet he cannot in his own strength break out of the spiritual gravity of his sinful nature, and get in touch and tune with God. He has no power over the thrust of temptation, the grip of sin, the approach of death and the certainty of judgment.'

There will be a day of judgment

The New Testament unwraps further what the consequences of turning from God are: 'Because of your stubbornness and your unrepentant heart, you are storing up wrath against yourself for the day of God's wrath, when his righteous judgment will be revealed. God will give to each person according to what he has done.'[8]

At one point in the American Civil War an average of 2,000 Union soldiers were dying every week. The bodies of these unfortunate victims were shipped north by train for proper burial. There were so many bodies that a new cemetery was needed. The responsibility for this was given to General Montgomery Meigs, whose own son had died in the battle of Shenandoah Valley. So great was his bitterness over this loss that General Meigs chose as the site the Virginia home of a Confederate officer. When the war was over, that officer, General Robert E. Lee, returned to his estate on the banks of the Potomac and saw that it had become Arlington National Cemetery, the Union Army's most hallowed ground. How ironic for Lee that so many of the young men killed by his forces were buried in his own front garden.

In a similar way the things that we do now are recorded and mount up. Our wrongdoings and failures are not forgotten, they are recorded, and will one day speak against us on the Day of Judgement. As the Bible puts it, we are 'destined to die once and after that to face judgment'.[9]

The last book of the Bible describes this event in these words:

> Then I saw a great white throne and him who was seated on it. Earth and sky fled from his presence, and there was no

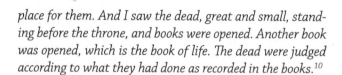

> *place for them. And I saw the dead, great and small, standing before the throne, and books were opened. Another book was opened, which is the book of life. The dead were judged according to what they had done as recorded in the books.*[10]

God is holy. The word 'holy' comes from the Hebrew and means 'to cut' or 'to separate'. God is in a very real sense totally other. Even though we are made in his image we are not God and never can be. He is different from us; he is totally holy and just. Even though he is love, his love does not lessen his holiness and justice. According to that holiness and justice, our guilt demands a response and that response is eternal punishment. God is bound by his very nature to punish sin — he would be inconsistent with himself if he did not. If God did not do this he would not be just, he would not be holy.

That's the bad news — but now for the good news.

The Good News

God is holy and just and is bound by his very nature to punish our sin, but he is also loving and merciful. How can the two be reconciled? How can God be just and loving? How can he be holy and merciful? How can he condemn our sin and yet forgive us? How can God's perfect justice and perfect love meet? The answer is in the death of Jesus on the cross.

On the cross Jesus took our punishment in our place. He was bearing what we should have borne. In Jesus, on the cross, God absorbed the offence and punishment for our wrongdoing himself. His justice is vindicated, and yet his mercy is shown.

The passion of the Christ

Mel Gibson's film *The Passion of the Christ* broke box office record records and at the same time ignited a storm of controversy over its extreme violence — and yet, with all this, it is easy to forget what the original event was all about.

This one incident is perhaps the most significant event of global history: it has radically changed the course of the world's unfolding drama and still shapes our global politics to this day. Present western secular society has grown out of, and in many senses has now reacted against, one and a half millennia of Christianity — all centred on conceptions of the cross of Christ. The United States, today's only superpower, has a government highly influenced by many politicians who believe it has momentous significance. Jews reject the crucifixion as the heretical and misleading mistake of a false Messiah, and Muslims militantly reinterpret it; they are vehemently antagonistic to the original meaning. Put all this together: the power of the secular West, along with the interactions of Muslims, Jews and Christians — and then centre them all around the city where it all took place, and you have the various scenarios we see in the news every day. The politics and power struggles of our world cannot be understood without reference to the so-called 'Passion of the Christ'. By ignoring, proclaiming, misconstruing and contradicting the affair of the crucifixion, communities often take their sides in our contemporary world.

But it is not just at the level of politics and ideology that this event is so relevant to the current situation: in a far more personal, emotional and experiential way, a vastly growing number throughout the planet testify that this one happening helps them make sense of their lives.

The trouble is, most people in the West have no idea whatsoever what it is all about — in our wholesale rejection of religion as outmoded and irrelevant, we have become blissfully ignorant of the crux of human history. We patronisingly reject things we are ignorant of.

So, in essence, what is Good News of the death of the Christ all about? Let me explain. The basic idea is incredibly simple and yet utterly radical and totally profound. Most religions believe in some ultimate being, and the big three, Judaism, Islam, and Christianity, teach that he is totally pure and righteous. If, for arguments sake, this is accepted, a key question arises — and one that is not merely theoretical; it is the question most people ask at one time or another. This key question is this: if God is totally pure and righteous, and I am aware of my moral failings in thought, attitude, motive, word and deed, then how can I ever be acceptable to him. If, as the Scriptures teach, God demands total perfection, then I am utterly lost. If heaven can only be entered by those who are perfect, then surely no one can enter it.

It is at precisely this point that the Christian conception is so different from all others. All the others teach in one way or another that we simply must try to be good enough, so that in the end our good deeds outweigh our bad. The Bible teaches that this is an impossibility, and for a couple of good reasons. First, no one has totally good deeds, all of our motives are mixed and are therefore not totally pure. Second, even if it was hypothetically possible for someone's good deeds to outweigh their bad, this would not solve the essential problem. If God is totally pure, the bad deeds, even if less than the good, are still sufficient to condemn us. God demands perfection — the good cannot undo the bad.

So, we have an immense and practical problem, how can we get rid of all the bad within us and so be acceptable to God? The Bible teaches that God is just and must punish all wrong, whether in thinking, attitudes or actions, and yet it also tells us that he is loving and wants to let us off, so to speak. How can God's justice and love be reconciled? How can the bad within us be justly dealt with? And this is where the death of Jesus comes in.

The amazing concept of the cross

Now comes the amazing concept of the cross, the idea that has revolutionized people's thinking and experience throughout the ages. The essential idea is this: when Jesus died on the cross, he was taking the punishment for our evil instead of us. Jesus became our substitute, sacrificing himself to pay the penalty for wickedness. Because he is Son of God, he is powerful enough to do this; because he is human he can legitimately represent us.

The astonishing upshot of all this is that forgiveness is possible for those who seek it; the past can be cleansed. And that is not just a religious thing; it has immense psychological significance. If God can forgive me, then I can forgive myself. Peace of mind is possible. And if this is true, then I can forgive others — and there is the possibility that they can forgive me. Here is the only basis for restitution and reconciliation at every level, from breakdown in marriages, all the way to tackling the legacy of the anguishing bloodbath that occurred in places like Rwanda and the Balkans.

In a world where feelings of guilt, breakdown in relationships, conflict between communities and all-out war are all around us, the possibility of personal forgiveness, as well as the basis to forgive others, is utterly vital.

Pictures in the Mind

In order to grasp more clearly the meaning of the cross of Christ it is helpful to have a look at some of the pictures that the Bible gives us to explain it. Because we tend to think in images this can be particularly valuable.

A picture of satisfaction

We are healed by the punishment he suffered.
(Isaiah 53:5)

A prairie fire is a horrifying thing. Towards the end of a long summer people on the scorched plains live in fear and suspense,

watching for any sign of haze or smoke. Once the tinder-dry vegetation has caught fire, swept by a breeze, everything in its broad path is consumed at frightening speed. Many have died in prairie fires.

But some have found a remarkably simple way of escape and have been saved from the advancing fire. They have gone out and set fire to a small area of grass and burned it off. Then they have taken refuge by standing where the fire has already been, knowing that the coming flames cannot touch them now.

Jesus has taken the fire of judgement in our place. When we turn to him for protection we are going to a place where the fire of God's righteous anger has already burnt. When we trust in Jesus Christ, we can approach a just and holy God because Jesus has taken the punishment for our sin in our place — God's totally justifiable and good anger against sin has been satisfied.

A picture of a ransom

Jesus came to 'give life as a ransom for many'.
(Mark 10:45)

During the American Civil War a band of Confederate soldiers were caught, but in the confusion of battle one managed to escape. The following day the prisoners were lined up in front of a firing squad. Without warning a young man ran into the camp, identifying himself as the one who had escaped. He pleaded with the Union Captain to let him take the place of an older family man, because he himself was single. The captain agreed and moments later the young man lay dead alongside his companions. One man walked out of the camp a free man, but not before he had erected a simple memorial engraved with his comrade's name and an inscription, 'He died in my place.' Jesus took the punishment for our failures instead of us.

On the cross Jesus said, 'It is finished.'[11] This phrase literally means 'the price is paid' and it was often used in the market-places of the time when the full cost of the goods bought was paid.

A picture of the law courts

But now a righteousness from God, apart from law has been made known ... This righteousness from God comes through faith in Jesus Christ to all who believe ... all have sinned and fall short of the glory of God, and are justified freely by his grace through the redemption that came by Jesus Christ.
(Romans 3:21-24)

Because of what Jesus has done on the cross we can be declared not guilty in the court of God's justice. In this way justice is not by-passed nor is the wrong trivialized. A full punishment is given but someone else takes it in our place.

Suppose someone without any money appears before a court for some crime and he is found guilty. The law requires the judge to impose a sentence, and he fines the man £500. The trouble is, the man can't pay; he is penniless. However, the judge is merciful as well as just. After delivering the sentence he comes down from the bench, walks over to the dock, takes out his chequebook and pays the culprit's fine. In this way justice and mercy are both satisfied; the law is not by-passed nor is mercy diluted.

A picture of a relationship

Through Christ, God was reconciling the world to himself.
(2 Corinthians 5:19)

Because of sin, people are separated and alienated from God — there is a barrier divorcing us from our Creator. Jesus' death on

the cross can mend our personal relationship with God; through it we can be forgiven and reconciled. This is sometimes called 'atonement', which comes from three Anglo-Saxon words added together: at-one-ment. Because of Jesus' death on the cross there can be an at-one-ment between God and us. Our relationship with God, once healed and restored, will never end. Even death will not stop it; it will last for ever.

A New Set of Clothes

Jesus did not merely take our badness, he also declared us good. It is not just that he has paid off our moral overdraft, but also that he filled our account with his righteousness. Someone once asked whether Jesus could have paid the price of our sins if he had died as an infant, like when Herod massacred the children of Bethlehem. The question is interesting because hidden within it is another question: why did Jesus have to live to adulthood in order to be able to give us forgiveness? Of course, if Jesus had died as a child we would not have his teaching or example, but more is at stake than this. Our problem before God is not merely that our sin has to be removed, but that we need to have righteousness credited to our account. It is not just that we need the penalty for breaking God's law taken from us, but also that we need to have obedience to the law given to us. We don't only need unrighteousness removed, but also positive righteousness needs to be credited to us. In the court of heaven we need to be declared forgiven and righteous. But righteousness is not merely not doing wrong, it is also positively doing good; it is not merely committing no sin, it is also actively achieving a perfectly righteous life. Righteousness is not only the absence of sin, it is also the presence of active obedience.

Jesus lived to adulthood so that he could grow up under the law and obey it in every single respect. Jesus was the perfect law keeper.[12] It is this law keeping or positive righteousness that is given to those who turn to Jesus. When believers approach God they are clothed or covered in the righteousness of Jesus Christ and so are fully acceptable.[13] Both the taking away of our sin by Christ's death and the covering of our shame by the righteousness of Christ's life are God's free gifts and cannot be earned or deserved.[14]

What Shall We Do?

About 2,000 years ago, just after these things originally happened, Peter, one of Jesus' disciples, spoke this message to the people of Jerusalem. His words had an amazing effect on them. 'When the people heard this, they were cut to the heart and said to Peter and the other apostles, "Brothers, what shall we do?"[15]

Peter replied, "Repent and be baptized, everyone of you, in the name of the Lord Jesus so that your sins may be forgiven. And you will be given the gift of the Holy Spirit. The promise is for you and your children and all who are far off — for all whom the Lord will call."'[16]

In many ways, we are the people who are 'far off'. Two thousand years later, in a different part of the world and in a very different culture, the message is still the same for us.

Jesus himself said,

For God so loved the world that he gave his one and only Son, that whoever believes in him shall not perish but have eternal life. For God did not send his Son into the world to condemn the world, but to save the world through him. Whoever believes in him is not condemned, but whoever does not believe stands condemned already because he has not believed in the name of God's one and only Son. This is the verdict: Light has come into the world, but men loved darkness instead of light because their deeds were evil. Everyone who does evil hates the light, and will not come into the light for fear that his deeds will be exposed. But whoever lives by the truth comes into the light, so that it may be seen plainly that what he has done has been done through God.[17]

Elsewhere, Jesus said, 'Ask and it will be given to you; seek and you will find; knock and the door will be opened to you. For everyone who asks receives; he who seeks finds; and to him who knocks, the door will be opened.'[18] Later, he went on, saying, 'Enter through the narrow gate. For wide is the gate and broad is the road that leads to destruction, and many enter through it. But small is the gate and narrow the road that leads to life, and only a few find it.'[19]

Postscript — A Health Warning

Having a mental makeover can feel very uncomfortable

Has what has gone before challenged your perceptions of the world you experience around you? If it has, this could produce a degree of psychological nausea, existential angst and emotional trauma. Put more simply, it could make you feel sick. You may feel confused.

If understood and taken on board, accepting what has been proposed here would be like experiencing a total mental makeover. There is the real risk of your view of everything being turned inside out and upside down. This is radical stuff.

Indeed, to use a more technical phrase, you may find your paradigm shifting — and nothing, absolutely nothing, can be more disorientating than that. Let me explain.

We have been on a mind-bending journey to uncover the ultimate secrets of the universe. In our thinking we have probed and prodded at the very fabric of reality as we have tried to answer its crucial question.

The Big Question has always been before us: Is there an ultimate being behind the universe that made it, upholds it and impregnates it with meaning? And then, can such a being be detected from the cosmos itself? Are there sufficient clues embedded in the matrix of reality as we perceive it that makes us look beyond it to a greater reality? And if such pointers do indicate God's existence, is it possible to know more about him than that he merely exists?

Like Alice on the way to her Wonderland, we have followed the White Rabbit down his burrow. For us, this burrow of all the causes and effects of the universe has led to a non-contingent, or independent cause. And then, as we considered the nature of the burrow, we became increasingly conscious that it is exceedingly complex, indeed, so complex it appears to be designed. But this was not all: the burrow has writing on its walls. The ultimate designer has left a message for mankind in the most remarkable document ever written — the Bible. And then, knowing that this was not enough, the great designer has stepped into the burrow, our dimension of time and space, to reveal himself yet more clearly.

The message he brings from that other eternal dimension is vital. It is crucial. The cosmos not only has physical laws of cause and effect, laws of chemistry and physics, it also has laws of morality. Together these constitute the Law of God. Weaved into the fabric of the burrow are the righteous and just requirements of the Lord God Almighty. If we break them, as we all do, an inviolable principle comes into effect that separates us from our Maker. And more frightening than that, we are answerable to him — we will be held to account for our thoughts, attitudes and actions. The universe has a judge. However, there is another principle that can intersect with this moral law: God can absorb all the pain and punishment of our breaking the ethical law in our place and provide us with his perfect righteousness as a gift to cover our moral nakedness. The separation between us and our Maker can be ended; the universe can make sense; life can have meaning. We can be at peace with God, ourselves, and the world.

For many, all this will feel like a totally alien view of everything. That is not surprising. We all think in terms of psychological models or frameworks; we have mental pictures that make sense to us. Philosophers of science have called these paradigms — they are the basic models that we fit our thoughts into. When we receive a new piece of knowledge we stick it into our old model, or paradigm. Indeed, the model controls our thinking; it is resistant to change. The history of science is littered with examples of where people were not convinced by new evidence, but hung screaming and kicking to their old familiar thought patterns and views. The flat earth believers were a particularly grim case in point. We are all resistant to changing our minds — we try to squeeze the new details into the old big picture. However, there is a time when this can become uncomfortable, very uncomfortable. Nothing seems to fit anymore. The old mental model can come under such stress that our belief in it is strained to breaking point; our paradigm begins to crack apart; thoughts start to lose their affinity for it and hunt for a new resting place. Atheism, agnosticism, naturalism, or whatever-ism can lose its attraction.

Gradually, or perhaps even suddenly, we can see things differently; a new centre of psychological gravity is formed; a new mental model, or paradigm, comes into being. Our thoughts reorient into a new thinking structure. The mental makeover begins and it is possible to have a fresh paradigm where all the details fit into a new framework.

This can all be very disorientating. As we start to dare to doubt whether the way we have always thought is possibly mistaken, we begin to feel that something, somewhere is wrong. As Morpheus said to Neo in the film *The Matrix*, 'There is a splinter in your mind that won't go away.' This splinter should not be ignored, but rather dealt with. The confusion and disorientation that are somewhat inevitable as old thinking is challenged should not be buried or avoided, but carefully and thoughtfully worked through.

The truth is out there — and it is worth seeking for.

Notes

Chapter 1: Follow the White Rabbit

1. The Greek philosopher Aristotle made the first main attempt to provide some kind of rational classic proofs for the existence of some kind of God, well before the time of Christ. These arguments were taken over and refined by possibly the most famous of the medieval theologians, Thomas Aquinas, in the thirteenth century. These classic arguments are expressed in a variety of ways, such as seeing God as the First Cause, the Prime Mover, or the Great Orderer, and are expressed most succinctly in what is known as Aquinas' Five Ways. They have been criticized over the years, most notably for attempting to prove too much in the use of the word 'prove', proving too little in that they only point to a philosophical abstraction called 'God' at best, and then that the arguments have inherent weaknesses, or have been made obsolete by scientific advances (like God being the Prime Mover — we now know that movement can be caused by some energy form other than movement). The first critique is dealt with here by, instead of using the word 'prove', to say that the evidence around us is 'consistent with' a belief in God. The God model is proposed as the best model. The second critique is dealt with in chapters 3 to 5 in showing that although arguments from the world around us do point to some powerful being that could be God (Psalm 19; Romans 1:20), they do not tell us much about this God. More is needed. To use theological jargon, general revelation can only go so far, special revelation is required to take us further. The third critique is answered by concentrating on the argument from contingency which avoids the criticisms. The weakness of the classic arguments is that they are in reality illustrations of an underlying argument. Because the illustrations at some point break down a weakness is seen. However, if one looks at the fundamental underlying argument that they are illustrating, it will be

found that that argument is immensely powerful. This underlying argument is the argument of contingency. That underlying argument is the one used here.

2. Spencer, Nick. *Beyond Belief? Barriers and Bridges in Faith Today*. London Institute of Contemporary Christianity. 2002.
3. This is often called 'Pantheism'.
4. As St Augustine said, 'Time is a property of the universe God created — there is no "before" creation.' Science may have come around to a Christian perspective.

Chapter 2: Down the Burrow

1. Davies, Paul. *God and New Physics*. Touchstone Books, p.188.
2. *Science of the Sacred*, Newsweek, 28 November, 1994.
3. Hawking, *A Brief History of Time*, p.139.
4. Hawking, *A Brief History of Time*, p.138.
5. Cited by John Polkinghorn, *One World*, SPCK, p.58.
6. Cited by John Blanchard in *Does God believe in Atheists*, Evangelical Press, p.272..
7. Cited by John Blanchard in *Does God believe in Atheists*, Evangelical Press, p.272.
8. Cited by David Wilkinson, *God, The Big Bang and Stephen Hawking*, Monarch Publications, p.108.
9. Stephen Hawking, *A Brief History of Time*, Bantam Books, 1995, p.139-140.
10. Quoted in, *The Wonders of God's Creation: Planet Earth*, Volume 1, (Chicago, Moody Institute of Science, 1993) videotape.
11. Cited by John Blanchard in *Does God Believe in Atheists*, Evangelical Press, p.283.
12. Michael J. Behe, *Darwin's Black Box*, Touchstone, 1998, p.x.
13. Michael J. Behe, *Darwin's Black Box*, Touchstone, 1998, p.232-233.

Chapter 3: The Voice

1. To the postmodernist who doubts whether language can communicate effectively, I would simply say that there is little point in making my case as, according to their viewpoint, they would not be able to comprehend what I say.

2. Kennedy, Ludovic, *All In The Mind: A farewell to God*, Hodder and Stoughton, 1999, p.xiii-xi.

3. Haldane, J.B.S. (Scottish mathematical biologist. 1892-1964), *Possible Worlds* (1927).

4. C. S. Lewis, *God in the Dock*, Grand Rapids, Eerdmans Publishing Company, 1970, p.53-53.

5. Darwin, C. 'Letter to W. Graham' in F. Darwin, ed., *The Life and Letters of Charles Darwin*. New York, D. Appleton & Co., 1905.

6. Of course, a Christian would also recognize that man's reason is not fool proof or unbiased. It is not utterly logical. Due to the Fall of humanity described in Genesis (Genesis 3) our thinking has become corrupted, and not only that, it also tends to be biased towards rejecting our Creator (Romans 1:18-23). This obviously does not mean that we have lost our ability to speak and reason though, for after the rebellion in the Garden of Eden God still speaks to Adam and expects him to understand and answer in words. God did not hear 'Oo oo ug ish' from behind the tree. Furthermore, he still expects us to understand the evidence around us that point to his existence and still holds us accountable when we reject this (Romans 1:18-20). Our mental software has become corrupted, but it has not crashed. Nevertheless, the fact that our ability to think even exists, even though corrupted, is entirely consistent with a belief in a creator God that made it, but also allowed it to become damaged as a result of our rebellion. This topic will be explored more fully in chapter 4, 'The Message'.

7. Numbers 22:38; Deuteronomy 18:18-20; Jeremiah 1:0; 14:14; 23:16-22; 29:31-32; Ezekekiel 2:7; 13:1-16.

8. 1 Kings 14:18; 16:12; 34; 2 Kings 9:36; 14:25; Jeremiah 37:2; Zechariah 7:7; 12.

9. Micah 3:8.

10. 2 Samuel 23:2.

11. 1 Corinthians 2:13.

12. 2 Timothy 3:16.

13. McAfee, Cleland B. *The Greatest English Classic*. New York, 1912, p.134.

14. Deuteronomy 18:21-22.

15. Micah 5:2.

16. Matthew 2:1; Luke 2:4-7.

17. Jeremiah 23:5.
18. Isaiah 9:1.
19. Psalm 22:16.
20. Isaiah 53:12.
21. Isaiah 53:11; Psalm 16:10.
22. Psalm 41:9.
23. Zechariah 11:12.
24. Zechariah 11:13b.
25. Zechariah 11:13b.
26. There is not sufficient room to set out the historical reliability of the Bible here. The reader should refer to the following texts: Josh McDowell, *Evidence that Demands a Verdict*, volumes 1 and 2. Paternoster Publishing, 1998; Charles F. Pfeiffer, ed. *Wycliffe Dictionary of Biblical Archaeology*. Hendrickson Publishers, 2000.

Chapter 4: The Word

1. John 1:1-18.
2. John 1:14.
3. Philippians 2:6-7.
4. 1 Peter 1:19.
5. 1 Peter 2:22.
6. 1 John 2:1.
7. 1 John 3:5.
8. Anderson, J.N.D. 'The Resurrection of Christ', *Christianity Today*, March 29, 1968, quoted in Josh McDowell, *Evidence that Demands a Verdict*, Volume 1, Paternoster Publishing, 1998 revised edition.
9. Mark 2:28; 9:9; 9:31.
10. Luke 22:70; Mark 3:11; Matthew 4:3, 6.
11. John 5:16-18.
12. Luke 22:66-71.
13. John 1:1.
14. He quoted it authoritatively (Matthew 4:4; Mark 14:27); he referred to it as the Word of God (Mark 7:11-13; John 10:34f); he believed the whole Old Testament to be authoritative (Luke 24:25-27) and he fulfilled it (Luke 24:25,27).
15. John 14:26.
16. John 16:13.

17. Matthew 28:16-20.

Chapter 5: The Word

1. Romans 1:20.
2. Genesis 2:16-17.
3. Genesis 3:7.
4. Genesis 3:6-24.
5. Romans 1:18-24.
6. This fits in with Satan's original temptation — Genesis 3:5.
7. Romans 3:23.
8. Romans 2:5.
9. Hebrews 9:27.
10. Revelation 20:11-13.
11. John 19:30.
12. Matthew 3:15; 5:17; Galatians 4:4 - 7; Romans 10:4; 2 Corinthians 5:21.
13. Just as God sacrificed an animal in the Garden of Eden to use its skin to cover Adam and Eve's shame and nakedness, so Christ's death allows his righteousness to covers our sin.
14. Ephesians 2:8.
15, Acts 2:37.
16, Acts 2:37-39.
17. John 3:16-21.
18, Matthew 7:7.
19. Mathew 7:13-14.

For More Information

http://theedgeofknownreality.com

Learn more about *The Edge*

Ask Jonathan Skinner a question

Listen to four radio programmes on the
contents of *The Edge* recorded with Trans
World Radio

Invite Jonathan to speak to your group

Find more resources